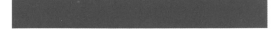
Coastal Corners of Cape Cod

Gil Newton

Published by Gilbert Newton
gdnewton@comcast.net
to benefit the Barnstable Land Trust

ISBN 978-0-9828122-5-9

To purchase a copy of this book, contact:
Barnstable Land Trust
407 North Street, Hyannis, Massachusetts 02601
508-771-2585 • www.BLT.org

Book produced by Nancy Viall Shoemaker, West Barnstable Press

Table of Contents

Acknowledgements

I am very grateful to the following individuals
for their assistance and support:

To **James R. Brown** and **Audrey F. Russano** for your
generous donation of your outstanding photographs.

To **Chris Dumas** whose excellent photography and
illustrations enhance the stories in this book.

To **Deborah Shiflett-Fitton**, fellow educator and Cape
Cod naturalist, for your wonderful introduction and
your commitment to the Cape's environment.

To **Nancy Viall Shoemaker** for your continuing
professional advice and guidance in the design and
creation of all my books.

This book is dedicated to
The Barnstable Land Trust.

Foreword

Observing, writing, communicating – these are the tools Gil Newton uses to encourage us to wade with him into his beloved marshes, transitional woodlands, dunes and mud flats of Cape Cod. He reaches out and encourages us to touch these special places, to understand their importance in our natural world, and to see our place in it.

Our changing shorelines and bordering ecosystems have no doubt been influenced by our human nature to live apart from our place in the natural world – the "real" world - and we are just beginning to see that this impact will be far reaching. The flora and fauna which surrounds us will change in order to adapt to rising sea levels, warming temperatures, and unpredictable weather patterns. Many will cease to exist on Cape Cod altogether. Will we miss their presence? Will we notice?

The first step to help quell these changes is to get in touch with our backyard – the corners of the Cape, and understand our place here. We need to feel the sand on our feet, the wind at our backs, and the smell of the salt in the air. We need to see the intricate beauty of seaweed, explore the wrack line at low tide, and understand the important value of eelgrass beds. We need to hear the many calls of the birds and watch their behavioral patterns as they move from ocean to shore, marsh to forest edge, north to south and back again on migration with the seasons. We need to understand the important role of the many fur-bearers who travel the ever dwindling wildlife corridors and frequent the shorelines to keep the fragile web of life in balance. From algae to grasses, insects to mollusks – they all play a part. Our job now is to reconnect with it all. If we are in touch with our natural world corners, we will understand the consequences of our actions. And Gil will help you understand your important role as a member of these wonderful fragile and changing ecosystems.

Enjoy your adventure with Gil as he brings the dynamic world of natural shoreline corners to life and to the forefront of our human daily experience here at home on Cape Cod.

Deborah Shiflett-Fitton
Field Biologist, Interpretive Naturalist and Science Educator
West Barnstable, MA

"Like so many before me,
I am attracted to wild, open spaces
that enchant and enrich."

Gil Newton

Observing the Coastline

The coastal environment is characterized by change. It is constantly re-formed and re-structured by waves, wind, and weather. And in this dynamic system one can find a wide variety of marine animal life. Many of these critters have evolved special adaptations to this hostile habitat while others float or wash in with the waves.

There is an adventure waiting for anyone who explores the coastal shoreline. Not every plant and animal is found distributed evenly throughout the shoreline. Living things are found in different habitats depending on their biological needs and physical requirements. For example a substrate may be sandy, rocky, muddy, pebbly or grainy. It may be protected in an inlet or bay or exposed to the open water and strong currents. It may be completely bare or covered by a thick patch of vegetation.

The chemistry of the water can vary also. In estuaries temperature, salinity, and dissolved oxygen may change drastically in 24 hours. The amount of sunlight as well as exposure at low tide can influence the arrangement of organisms along the shore. Waves, currents, storms, and even other animals (through predation and competition) can alter the distribution of life at a marine habitat.

To begin any study of nature, put together a field notebook. Recording your observations at the time you're outside will help you identify any unknown organisms you encounter. Subtle, daily changes can also be recorded such as the tides, weather and sediment type.

Start by gathering some simple materials including a small notebook, pencil, plastic metric ruler, and a hand lens. Select an area that can be observed throughout the different seasons. Describe the habitat and make a brief sketch of the area. Try to be as specific as possible. If you are interested in identifying any species without collecting it, make a sketch of the plant or animal and measure its size, color, shape and condition.

One of the most valuable ways of learning about any critter is to keep a journal or log of observations and sketches. This is particularly beneficial over a long period of time in which changes in the habitat can be recorded as well as notations on specific growth and development. Living things should be observed during different seasons, time of day, and weather conditions. The area you select for a long-term study should be relatively undisturbed. Also, before you use a field guide for identifications, test your own powers of observation. This may actually save you a lot of time from thumbing through a book and looking at dozens of pictures.

There are several questions that you can explore. Do the plants and animals in this area have similar characteristics? Are there variations within the population of the same organism? How are they distributed on the beach?

Another related experiment is to compare different plots in the region. Comparing one sample plot to another can show changes that have taken place, a phenomenon known as succession. Each organism within the plot has certain soil, light and space requirements. Usually these plots are made in units of square meters, but any size can be studied.

Start by marking and measuring the area with string or ribbon. An easy plot to measure is a square of one meter by one meter for each species. In your field notebook write the symbol for each organism you see in the plot. How are they distributed within the plot? Would you describe them as random, clumped, or uniform?

Now count the number of individuals for each species. This tells you the density of the organism per meter squared. Mark out another nearby plot and make the same calculations. Compare the two plots. How do they differ? What environmental conditions allow some to live in the plot and not others?

You may want to collect some of the algae to prepare a plant collection. Dried and pressed specimens can be mounted and labeled on paper. Known as a herbarium, this collection of specimens should remain in excellent condition for many years. Collect some seawater along with the specimen. At home use a large pan or tray to float the  algae. Place a thick sheet of paper under the plant in the tray. Use official herbarium stock, oak tag, or a large index card. Slowly raise the paper so that the plant is picked up. Then carefully drain the excess water from the paper. You can arrange the seaweed branches by using a medicine dropper. Cover the plant with cheese cloth or wax paper and place between several sheets of newspaper. Finally place some large books or heavy objects on the newspaper and change the paper the next day. After two to three days you can peel the cheese cloth or wax paper away and the seaweed will remain stuck to the paper.

Beachcombing can be a very entertaining and interesting activity at any coastline. Shells, beach glass, drift wood, seaweed, and small animals are frequently found. Keeping records of these finds can be equally interesting and informative for they will document the dynamic nature of the beach. Seasonal changes, storm activity, and the movement of animals along the intertidal zone will result in a constantly changing ecosystem. It's fun to observe and monitor these changes and to appreciate the diversity of marine life along the shore.

Two Field Trips

There are many wonderful and interesting beaches on Cape Cod. The Cape's economy is largely dependent on its coastal resources from tourism to fishing. For those of us who live here, there are a few special places that have great meaning. We may have had a personal experiencc with these special places. One of my favorites is Dowses Beach in Osterville, a small barrier beach system surrounded by Nantucket Sound on one side and East Bay on the other.

I have taken many of my students on their first field trip to this lovely beach. From a coastal ecology point of view the area is interesting because it can be divided into a series of interdependent mini habitats. Collectively they make up the area we call Dowses, but each one can be studied for its own unique assemblage of plants and animals as well as specific physical characteristics.

Start off with the small dune system dividing both sides of the parking lot. There are several species here including beach grass (*Ammophila breviligulata*), seaside rose (*Rosa rugosa*), seaside goldenrod (*Solidago sempervirens*), and wormwood (*Artemisia caudata*). Small mammals, insects and birds congregate here. And it's the favorite habitat of the dreaded deer tick (*Ixodes scapularis*). You can observe some small unvegetated and open areas of the dune called blow-outs where the wind removes the sand, creating passages for wildlife and for nesting areas for piping plovers.

The sandy beach is characterized by a distinct wrack line where the remains of slipper snails (*Crepidula fornicata*) exist by the hundreds. Scallop shells, mole crabs, and jingle shells are found here. Signs of eelgrass beds are seen and the dominant and invasive *Codium* green seaweed washes up in enormous quantities.

A rock jetty connects the bay to the open water and barnacles (*Semibalanus balanoides*), rockweed (*Fucus vesiculosus*), and

periwinkle snails (*Littorina littorea*) are living in patchy zones on the jetty. The surfaces of some of the rocks are smooth while others are coated with a slick film of green algae and bacteria. Across the bay one can observe much of the sand eroded by the jetty that has been deposited on the other side. Terns and plovers have established residency there.

fiddler crab

Continuing towards the bay side one encounters a small mud flat where many periwinkles gather and where several red seaweeds wash ashore. The bay is quieter with less wave and wind activity and we often find the remains of blue (*Callinectes sapidus*), spider (*Libinia emarginata*), and hermit (*Pagurus longicarpus*) crabs. The bay is surrounded by a ring of salt marsh with its distinct *Spartina* grasses and evidence of fiddler crab (*Uca pugnax*) homes.

Finally the tour is complete with a quick visit to a salt pond connected to the system via a culvert under the entrance road. This pond can be stagnant with algae blooms occurring in the summer. Still there are many ribbed mussel (*Modiolus demissus*) beds in the banks and small groups of mallard ducks (*Anas platyrhynchos*) living there.

This brief tour shows clearly that, in a dynamic beach system such as Dowses, all of its sections are interconnecting and ecologically important. While constantly changing, each mini habitat influences all the others and supports a sustainable and productive ecosystem.

Dowses Beach is a popular recreational resource in Barnstable. But Cape Cod is also home to a very popular national park. The Cape Cod National Seashore is visited by over four and one-half million people each year. This beautiful park consists of thousands of acres of diverse habitats including spectacular beaches, three widely used bicycle trails, and eleven magnificent self-guiding trails to use and enjoy.

One of these trails is located in Wellfleet and extends for about a mile. Going through a series of terrestrial transition zones, the trail intersects the largest Atlantic White Cedar Swamp on Cape Cod which is several acres in size. The swamp was formed around 7,000 years ago after the glaciers retreated. The Cape's ponds, swamps and freshwater marshes are the results of the scouring and subsequent melting of these glaciers. Over time the plant life decomposed and formed large layers of peat. These layers can be helpful in determining the age of the swamp. Because these bodies of freshwater represent the surface layer of groundwater, one can visit the swamp and estimate the status of the water table. During years of drought I have seen this swamp completely dry. There have been times when it was difficult to convince my students that this is indeed a swamp.

White Cedar Swamp photos: Nancy Viall Shoemaker

Park officials have cut and marked this trail through a remarkable diversity of habitats. Near the ocean the pitch pines (*Pinus rigida*) and scrub oaks (*Quercus ilicifolia*) are sharply reduced in size due to the influence of salt spray and wind. As the trail winds down to the swamp, the vegetation changes from a mixed coniferous woodland to very tall white (*Quercus alba*) and black (*Quercus velutina*) oaks which dominate the area at the furthermost point from the ocean. All along the edge are small plants such as bearberry (*Arctostaphlos uva-ursi*), wintergreen (*Gaultheria procumbens*), and broom crowberry (*Corema conradii*) that thrive in acidic, sandy conditions.

An interesting phenomenon takes place around the edge of the swamp just before the boardwalk begins. A population of red maple (*Acer rubrum*) trees surrounds the swamp. This tree is competitive with the Atlantic white cedar (*Chamaecyparis thyoides*), though its root system is unable to tolerate very wet conditions. The red maple survives better in dry years and can shade out the white cedars.

The trail is lined with many groundcover species including broom crowberry (*Corema conradii*), bearberry (*Arctostaphylos uva-ursi*), and wintergreen (*Gaultheria procumbens*). Large mats of these evergreen species are also found on the nearby dunes in the Marconi area. They produce many berries to help support the abundant animal populations at the edge of the woods.

8

Where the Critters Are

There are numerous unique and ecologically significant relationships between living things in the marine environment. They often involve the movement or transfer of energy from one organism to another. These complicated marine food webs are rich in productivity and are responsible for most of the photosynthetic activity on earth. Without these systems life in the terrestrial environment would not exist.

Even in a hostile environment, such as the intertidal zone of a sandy beach, life can be present. Most of the organisms here have adapted to a burrowing existence. Small clams, mole crabs, and annelid worms live in the substrate and must survive varying physical conditions. Wave action, sand particle size, and oxygen concentration will affect the distribution of life in this dynamic environment.

The water column is characterized by a large diversity of microscopic plant and animal plankton, at least in the upper 100 meters where light can penetrate. There can be thousands of single-celled algae present, all photosynthesizing and providing the earth with most of its oxygen supply, as well as marine animals with the energy needed to sustain their populations. Because of the size of the ocean and the abundance of algae, these species account for more than three-quarters of all plant life on earth.

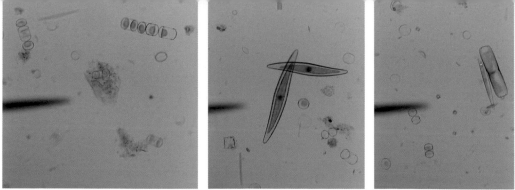
phytoplankton (diatoms)

All plants and animals have evolved strategies for survival and adaptations to the environment. In the case of phytoplankton, many species form chains or have appendages that enable them to float closer to the surface where there is ample sunlight for photosynthesis. Some animal species such as marine crabs and sea stars can regenerate or replace lost limbs which grow back after a short period of time. The burrowing fiddler crab can breathe in water but can also store oxygen in gill chambers. Barnacles use their six pairs of legs to beat in the water and push food into their mouths. They are able to close up for protection from desiccation at low tide.

Rock jetties are interesting coastal habitats to explore. These structures may contain a wide diversity of living organisms that have adapted to the harsh conditions of constant wave, tide, and storm activity. The most conspicuous inhabitants of this habitat are the common rockweeds (*Fucus vesiculosus* and *Ascophyllum nodosum*), brown algae that can survive periodic exposure to the air at low tide. Hiding underneath their fronds are bands of small animals such as barnacles, periwinkles and crabs.

However, these plants and animals are not distributed evenly along the jetty. Some of the rocks might be completely devoid of all life, while others have smaller, more randomly distributed populations. This variation, called patchiness, is caused by several physical and biological factors.

The most important physical influence occurs on the side directly facing the waves and tides. Obviously strong wave action will limit the colonization and growth of any critter trying to get established. Even those already present could be removed by strong wave energy from a storm.

There are also many less visible interactions between the different life forms present. Because of the limited surface area on the rocks, there is competition for that valuable real estate.

Some species may only occupy a small portion of the rocks because they are unable to survive prolonged periods of exposure. Some may seek shelter under the seaweed fronds to avoid predators.

Rockweed can also influence colonization rates. The movement of water causes this seaweed to sway back and forth. This motion can brush away any larvae attempting to attach to the rock surface. Other plants and animals may be subject to grazing pressures. Some habitats on Cape Cod contain huge numbers of periwinkle snails which normally graze on small algae on the rocks and seaweed. But if their numbers get too high, they may start to consume the rockweed and limit its growth. This process of succession is not always predictable and may vary from one rock interface to another. Sometimes it's just a matter of who gets there first.

Another coastal habitat worth examining for different critters is the wrack line at the high tide mark. Carefully sorting through the seaweed and eel grass can reveal many species tangled in this mat. There are often several species that are attached or encrusted on the algae. This tiny world is often overlooked at the beach. Yet these creatures are important links in the marine food web.

It's always fun and exciting to find something rare and unusual along the beach. By exploring specific habitats, a wider diversity of marine life forms can be located and studied.

Flotsam and Jetsam of the Wrack Line

At the high water mark along a sandy beach there is a row of debris left behind when the waves recede. This is known as the wrack line and is an interesting area to explore. Wrack refers to the common brown seaweed knotted wrack (*Ascophyllum nodosum*) which sometimes makes up the majority of the plant material. However, there are several other species that may be present in abundance.

I've seen wrack lines in which eelgrass (*Zostera marina*), a true flowering plant, dominates the assemblage. The oyster thief (*Codium fragile*) is also part of this debris in areas where it is invasive. Other algae species may include *Sargassum* (Gulf weed), *Fucus* (rockweed), and *Chondrus* (Irish moss). These species are left high and dry and will decompose on the beach forming an organic layer of detritus. A wrack line is the classic example of flotsam and jetsam and is a diverse and fascinating microhabitat on the beach.

When observing and examining a wrack line one should wear heavy garden gloves as this is an area that accumulates human debris as well including sharp objects like broken glass.

Under the fronds of seaweed you may find a large population of beach fleas, also called sand hoppers (*Talorchestia longicornis*). These animals are not insects but are crustaceans in a group called amphipods. They get their common names because they will jump or hop in the wrack. They will scavenge through the seaweed feeding on bits of detritus.

The largest marine snails in the northeast are the whelks. The two most common are the channeled whelk (*Busycon canaliculatum*) and the knobbed whelk (*B. carica*) The major difference  between them is that the latter has small knobs on the outside of the shell. What you are most likely to find are their egg cases. These are long strings of brown parchment cases which may still contain dozens of tiny unhatched whelks.

Another egg case which gets entangled in the wrack line is commonly called the mermaid's purse. This once encased a young skate which is a cartilaginous fish related to sharks. The case has a black square center with a pair of prongs at each end. It is also called the devil's purse. Chances are that you will collect an empty egg case in which the young skate has already hatched out.

The sponge deadman's fingers (*Haliclona occulata*) can be found in the wrack line after a storm. This yellowish sponge may produce a few branches and, like other sponges, it has no organs or organ systems. When alive the red beard sponge (*Microciona prolifera*) is bright red with many branches. However it quickly loses its color after it dies and is often collected in a brown form.

One of the shells you might find by the hundreds belongs to the slipper snail (*Crepidula fornicata*). It can also be seen in large heaps attached to one another. The larger snails at the bottom of the pile are the females and the smaller ones at the top are males. The animal is easily identified by the presence of a small indentation or platform along the opening of the shell.

One unusual specimen that can be found here is the red alga, *Corallina officinalis*, also called coral weed. This alga has the ability to remove calcium carbonate (lime) from the water and encase itself in a hard white coating. When the plant dies, it looks like tiny bones when examined under a hand lens or microscope. Even though it may be covered with lime, it can still photosynthesize, though probably at a reduced rate. Possibly this adaptation helps reduce herbivory by grazing animals.

Also in the wrack line is the interesting animal *Bugula turrita*, a bryozoan that looks like brown bushy seaweed. Don't be fooled because this is an animal that attaches itself to shells, rocks and seaweed and can foul the bottom of boats. Use a hand lens to distinguish it from the algae.

Coastal Corners of Cape Cod

A real surprise and treat is to find the presence of coral. Though there are no coral reefs in the northeast, there is an animal here called star coral (*Astrangia dannae*) which can be white to pinkish and can form thin crusts on rocks and shells. I have found it washed up in the wrack line on the beaches in Woods Hole. Like other corals, it consists of several individuals in a colony.

Undoubtedly the wrack line will also consist of pieces and body parts of dead animals. Crab claws and legs, broken shells, horseshoe crab molts, and stranded jellyfish all get entangled in the seaweed that marks the upper tide mark. Driftwood, beach glass, and plastic debris will also be seen in this area.

star coral

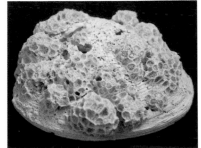

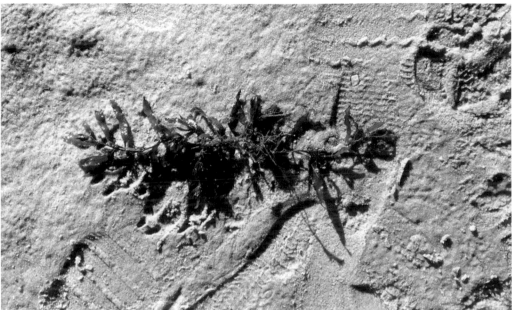

Sargassum

The Aesthetics of Seaweed

My interest in marine algae has always been primarily scientific. The diversity of forms, the complex life cycles, and their environmental importance has great appeal to me. Yet I would be remiss if I didn't say that I find them as attractive and beautiful as others may feel about orchids, roses, or lilies. I have prepared hundreds of specimens for my classes and studies and there is no outdoor activity that I enjoy more than scanning the Cape's beaches, marshes, and rock jetties in search of rare specimens of green, brown, or red algae.

By far my favorite seaweed is the strangely shaped and somewhat elusive brown alga, *Leathesia difformis*, commonly called the sea potato. It's one of the easiest seaweeds to identify, characterized by being hollow, spherical, and rubbery. It goes by other descriptive names as well including rat's brain and sea cauliflower. It is approximately three to five inches in size, depending on its age. Normally it is found washed up on the beach during the warmer summer months. It disappears in the winter as it enters its microscopic stage. Its range is quite extensive and can be found from Canada to the Carolinas. There are many locations on Cape Cod where the sea potato can be spotted.

This alga is a member of the brown algae group and its color is due to the pigment fucoxanthin which masks the chlorophyll pigments that enable it to make its own food through photosynthesis. While the sea potato may be unfamiliar to most, it belongs to the same group of algae that includes the common rockweeds and kelps. The sea potato is epiphytic which means that it grows on other seaweeds, particularly the common red alga Irish moss (*Chondrus crispus*). I have also collected it growing on the flowering marine plant eel grass (*Zostera marina*). However, it is typically seen isolated from its host when found on a beach. I am always searching for it when I'm beachcombing, but sometimes with little success. In fact, it appears when and where I least expect it.

sea potato

My most successful collecting trip occurred at the barrier beach system of South Cape Beach in Mashpee, Massachusetts. I took my coastal ecology class from the Cape Cod Community College. We found dozens of specimens in a small area. The round, yellowish-brown sea potatoes are sometimes tangled with other plants and shells in the wrack line. However, there have been many visits in which our search came up empty. After a series of field trips to this beach without finding any samples, I offered an automatic A on the field report to any student who could locate a sea potato. I should have conducted the inspection first. We weren't there for more than a minute before several students came up to me with handfuls of sea potatoes. Grades were good for that class.

We took our collection back to the classroom lab for closer examination. The students commented on the gelatinous and spongy nature of the algae. We cut small, thin sections of the seaweed and looked at them under a microscope, revealing a mass of thread-like filaments. Because of its round shape it was difficult to make a pressed specimen for the herbarium, so I preserved it in a jar of formalin. Unfortunately most of the pigment faded when treated this way.

Sometimes I think that my students get a kick out of seeing my reaction to a successful seaweed hunt. Once I took a couple of Sandwich High School students to Sandwich Town Neck Beach where we quickly found several sea potatoes. I was jumping up and down with excitement as I had never found my favorite seaweed at that location before. I explained the unique biology of the sea potato to the two kids and told them how lucky they were to see this. Out of the corners of my eyes I could see them rolling theirs.

The rockweeds are also another fascinating group of brown algae. The large populations of *Fucus* on jetties and in salt marshes are homes to many living things. This can be observed at low tide in a marsh. The *Fucus* that grows along the banks forms a canopy layer that protects many animal species underneath. Because *Fucus* contains a coating of mucilage, it retains its moisture and prevents desiccation of other marine organisms. Embedded in the banks under the *Fucus* canopy are clusters of ribbed mussels. Barnacles, bryozoans, worms, crabs and periwinkle snails may also be present. The rockweed provides them with a layer of protection from predators and gives them a substrate for their larva and eggs.

Fucus

Rockweed is an important habitat for other animals as well. Several species of juvenile fish such as winter flounder can occupy a rockweed community. Even shorebirds can be seen foraging in the rockweed, feeding on mollusks and crustaceans. There is a small polychaete tube worm called *Spirorbus* which grows its white circular tubes on the fronds of *Fucus vesiculosus*.

Animals such as sea stars are attracted to this community and feed on the abundant mussels present. Another echinoderm, the sea urchin, can be found here particularly if there are kelp algae growing with the rockweed.

The life cycle of *Fucus* is very interesting. The brown branches split in the form of a Y. Small, spherical structures called conceptacles form near the receptacles or the end tips of the branches. Looking like small swollen bumps, these structures function in the reproduction of this alga. The male structure is called the antheridium and releases the motile, haploid sperm cells into the water. The female structure is the oogonium. It releases the haploid egg cells which are carried by water currents. A single sperm cell will fertilize an egg cell resulting in a floating diploid zygote. Eventually the zygote settles down on a suitable surface such as a rock jetty and grows into an adult alga.

One of the most interesting aspects to this life cycle is that there are no spores produced, unlike many other marine algae. Also this process is not as random as originally thought. In rough waters the alga rarely gives up its gametes (sperm and eggs). During calm seas the amount of carbon dioxide needed for photosynthesis is reduced, triggering the release of the gametes which increases the success rate of fertilization. *Fucus* can also reproduce throughout the year.

The life cycle of the knotted wrack (*Ascophyllum nodosum*) is very similar. Like *Fucus* the gametes are produced in male and female conceptacles on the tips of branches in the spring. The receptacles take on a yellowish tinge and the eggs and sperm are released into the water column where fertilization takes place. Following this a zygote forms and settles on a substrate where it grows into the diploid alga.

This form of sexual reproduction is called oogamy and is seen in the Fucales. However one of the rockweeds, *Sargassum*, may also reproduce asexually or vegetatively by fragmentation in which small pieces of the alga can grow directly into adults.

Rockweeds are used economically in many industries. Because of their unique chemistry these algae are considered valuable in agriculture and industry. Rockweed can be used to fertilize and enhance soil condition. Faster and stronger root and stem growth occurs with the application of seaweed. Knotted wrack is the most widely used rockweed in this way. It contains many minerals, vitamins and hormones that increase root growth when applied in the form of an extract.

Rockweeds also contain the polysaccharide alginate which can be used as a stabilizer in foods such as ice cream or in cosmetics such as a skin moisturizer. Rockweeds can also be nutritional additives in pet and livestock food. They are rich in both macronutrients (nitrogen, potassium, and phosphorus) and micronutrients (iron, copper, and zinc). *Fucus vesiculosus* is the original source of commercial iodine which was widely used to treat thyroid conditions.

The red algae are often cited as the prettiest of the seaweeds. Chenille weed (*Dasya pedicellata*) has many fine, tiny hairs along the branches which can be seen with a hand lens. It is very delicate and gives a feathery appearance when under water. Another red alga that catches the eye is Grinnell's pink leaf (*Grinnellia americana*). The name describes it perfectly. It looks like a thin pink

leaf. Some of the blades have spots on them which are reproductive spores. Another common red alga that is interesting because of its appearance is coral weed (*Corallina officinalis*). This small, jointed seaweed seems to be encased in a hard, white coating of lime or calcium carbonate. It is somewhat purplish when alive and all white when dead.

coral weed

One of the most common examples of marine red algae is also one of the most complex. A genus called *Polysiphonia* is often seen attached to small rocks, shells, and other algae species in the intertidal zone. This attractive seaweed appears to have bands along its central branch. These are actually groups of pericentral cells and are seen on all branches. Like other marine algae, *Polysiphonia* photosynthesizes, but it also contains the red pigment phycobilin which gives the alga its characteristic color.

The life cycle of *Polysiphonia* is amazingly complicated for such a small ancient organism. The plant collected in the field may be the tetrasporophyte stage which releases a series of tetraspores. These germinate into either a male or female gametophyte plant. The male produces the spermatangia and the female forms a structure called a cystocarp that is fertilized by a single spermatium. After this occurs another kind of spore, the carpospores, forms and develops into the tetrasporophyte again.

Three are hundreds of species of *Polysiphonia* world wide and around a dozen in the Cape Cod region. Some of these are epiphytes, growing on other plants. One of the most interesting *Polysiphonia* epiphytes is *P. lanosa* which grows exclusively on the brown knotted wrack *Ascophyllum nodusum. P. lanosa* is a small bushy alga growing in clumps on the branches of *Ascophyllum*.

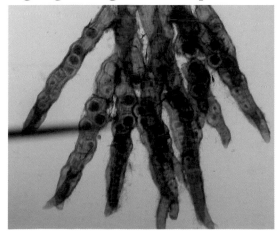

Possibly it's more resistant to desiccation than other species or maybe it is able to increase its rate of photosynthesis by floating to the surface because of *Ascophylum's* large air bladders. It can be spotted and identified with a good hand lens.

Locating smaller seaweeds such as *Polysiphonia* requires patience and close examination of shallow waters. There are many tiny, almost obscure plants and animals which remain hidden under shells or larger seaweeds. I sometimes carry a bucket with me, collect a clump of macroalgae, and take it back to the lab. I then spread the collection into large trays where the material can be more closely examined.

Irish moss

Other attractive red algae include some very useful species. The next time you eat ice cream or brush your teeth with toothpaste or paint your living room, keep in mind that you might be using a product that has seaweed in it. That is you might be using an extract from seaweed called carrageenan. Most likely this came from a red alga including a common one that grows in many parts of the world, namely Irish moss (*Chondrus crispus*).

Irish moss grows in large populations and is attached to rocks and the substrate by a small disc-shaped holdfast. This alga is deeply red to purple though it may be yellowish-green if exposed to direct sunlight for long periods of time. The blades are up to four inches long and dichotomously branched. It usually grows in the lower portions of the intertidal zone.

Irish moss is a red alga and not a moss. It was a staple of the Irish diet during the potato famine and Irish immigrants were the first to harvest it in Massachusetts. A large mossing industry

22   **Coastal Corners of Cape Cod**

developed in Scituate, Massachusetts in the mid-1800's and continued through World War II. The harvesting of Irish moss using long iron rakes was another way of earning a living by the sea. Even today a seaweed pudding is made using Irish moss along with some milk, sugar, salt and vanilla extract.

There are many commercial and industrial uses of carrageenan. A partial list includes yogurt, beer, puddings, fruit juice, cake batter, pie fillings, and cottage cheese. The thickening agent present prevents ice crystal formation in ice cream. It's also used in some medicines, cosmetics, paints, body lotions, and paper production.

Irish moss has an extensive distribution and grows abundantly along the Atlantic coastline in North America and Europe. There are several related species found in the Pacific Ocean. It has also been collected in the Mediterranean and Bering Seas. Its appearance may vary from place to place depending on wave action.

The world of marine algae is endlessly fascinating for many scientific reasons, but we cannot overlook the fact that algae are also among the most aesthetically pleasing marine inhabitants when seen in their natural habitats.

Codium

The Oyster Thief

One of the most invasive seaweeds is the green alga *Codium fragile*, subspecies tomentosoides, also called the oyster thief and dead man's fingers. This introduced species originated from Asia, most likely Japan. It might have arrived on these shores by attaching to ships or possibly oyster shells from Europe where it was also introduced. The young plants can attach to practically any hard surface including rocks, nets, and shells. That's part of the problem. It can also be very damaging to shellfish beds. *Codium* can grow over the filter feeding siphons of clams and block them. It can also weigh down the motile scallops, preventing them from feeding. *Codium* can be very thick and bushy so that a smaller attached clam or scallop can be removed from its natural habitat by floating away with the seaweed.

Codium can also harm shellfish indirectly, particularly in valuable eel grass beds offshore. *Codium* gets so thick that it blocks sunlight to the eel grass, thus reducing its ability to photosynthesize and provide food to the numerous animals that live there. If *Codium* gets established in aquaculture beds, it can sharply reduce productivity.

Codium is easy to identify. Branches are bright green and spongy in their texture. A thick, flat, root-like structure at its base, called a holdfast, attaches to different objects such as clams, snails, and rocks. The alga can reproduce quickly and abundantly through a vegetative process called fragmentation. Small pieces can break off from the adult plant and grow into new ones. It's this ability to fragment that makes it so difficult to control. It can also reproduce through a process of parthenogenesis. In this species swimming female cells called gametes are released into the water, attach to a hard surface, and grow into a new plant without fertilization from a male cell.

All invasive species have certain characteristics in common. They can reproduce quickly and in large numbers. Some can reproduce in more than one way. They often grow and live in a wide range of environmental conditions including temperature and salinity. They can adapt to a new environment with little competition.

Codium has adapted to the waters of Cape Cod and is mainly found in the warmer water on the southern side of the Cape. It has fouled many beaches and appears to be increasing in population. So what can be done to control it? Unfortunately, very little has been successful. Unlike the more notorious invasive plant, *Phragmites*, *Codium* has not received the same amount of attention. The manual removal of the massive amounts along the beaches has been the most commonly used method. Controlling nitrogen loading into bays and estuaries will also help. Some parts of the world harvest *Codium* as a source of fertilizer, even food. I've used it in my garden as an inexpensive source of compost material. At any rate, this invasive alga deserves our attention for the simple reason that it is already having a negative impact on the financially important shellfish industry, as well as the visual enjoyment of many of the Cape's beaches.

Plant Invaders

One of the disturbing trends in plant ecology is the reduction in diversity and the increase in the distribution of invasive species. From the sandy beaches and dunes to the open fields and meadows to the mixed pine and oak forests, there are several species that dominate the landscape at the expense of a greater variety of plants.

These plant invaders all have certain features in common. They are well adapted to a wide range of environmental conditions, often flourishing in poor soils and periods of drought. They may have structural features which increase their adaptation success, such as a long taproot, or a very high seed production. They can grow through more than one season, and quickly outcompete rival plants for space, water, and nutrients. Some easily displace other plants by growing vegetatively through a strong underground stem or rhizome, while others may release chemicals into the soil that block the growth of other plants.

Some plants with invasive tendencies are referred to as weeds. This designation suggests wind pollination, growth in disturbed areas, and a lack of herbivores that could control the spread of the weed. Their competitive nature really gives them an edge. Very few species can get a foothold when confronted with *Phragmites*, greenbrier, spotted knapweed, or the multiflora rose.

Phragmites

One plant invader that elicits mixed feelings is the common greenbrier (*Smilax rotundifolia*), also called bullbrier. This frequently seen plant can grow profusely around the edges of salt marshes and forms huge thick stands that are nearly impossible to walk through. Though native, it has easily spread because of the altered landscape in this area.

The leaves are simple, alternate, and heart-shaped and may remain on the shrub into the winter. It has a wide tolerance for different soil types and pH and can spread quite easily, like so many other plant invaders, via an underground rhizome. Having thorns and tendrils, this species can climb trees and form a thicket that quickly overcomes other species. The thorns allow the plant to cling to other branches while the tendrils wrap around them, enabling the greenbrier to spread in several directions. Even if cut or burned, growth is stimulated and occurs from the rhizome.

The plant's small cluster of flowers can be seen during the summer. The fruits which follow are bluish-black berries that linger throughout the winter. The seeds are spread by animals that feed on the berries, thus increasing the plant's range.

The largest populations of greenbrier that I have observed occur along the edges of woodlands and open fields. These thickets tend to grow inwards, adding another layer of shrubbery that blocks the growth of smaller herbaceous plants. I've also noticed thick stands of greenbrier on the upland portions of salt marshes.

Unlike many of the plant invaders, greenbrier has some significant ecological value. The plant provides important shelter and nesting sites for many animals. Its berries provide nourishment to several common animals such as cardinals, cedar waxwings, catbirds, wild turkeys, raccoons, and squirrels. White-tailed deer graze on its leaves. Many insects can be found in a greenbrier patch as well.

The problem is, of course, its aggressive nature. Its negative impact on plant biodiversity might actually reduce its value as a wildlife plant. Predators may have a difficult time negotiating the sharply thorned branches. Greenbrier tends to block out sunlight for other plants to grow. Other plant species may also support many animals in a variety of ways. So the presence of greenbrier is not necessarily a negative for the environment, but when it grows to the point of completely colonizing an area, it can become a major pest.

The most effective means of controlling this species is mechanical removal of the entire plant, including its rhizome and root system. Unfortunately, that task must be accomplished early and thoroughly if it is to succeed.

There is a plant invader that takes many forms and should be avoided wherever possible. The plant is poison ivy (*Toxicodendron radicans*) and it can be found growing as an herb, shrub, or vine. It grows in woodlands, the edges of lawns, on sand dunes, and up tall trees. I have even seen it growing on a mound of land in the middle of a salt marsh. All parts of the plant contain the toxin urushiol and can cause severe dermatitis if contacted.

Fortunately this is an easy plant to spot, particularly in the summer and early fall. Look for a plant with three leaflets attached to the petiole. The leaves are usually bright green, but can turn red in the fall. Yellow flowers appear in late spring through mid-summer, and small, round gray fruits appear in clumps on the plant from late summer through the winter.

Winter identification is a bit trickier. After the plant loses its leaves, it forms a curved terminal bud. Look for this marking, especially when walking through the woods. While it is less likely that you will contract the dermatitis in the winter, it is still possible.

Contact with the poison can occur directly or indirectly. If you touch any part of the plant that has been broken, the sap can penetrate your skin and itching and a rash will occur shortly afterwards. Of course any pet can also pick up the sap and you may become infected by touching its fur. There have also been cases where individuals have been infected by the burning of plants. Small particles of urushiol can be disseminated in the air and exposure can even occur internally. That is one of the reasons why burning poison ivy is a risky form of control.

Some people are so highly allergic to poison ivy however, that removal of it is sometimes necessary. I know of one case of a homeowner who lived near a dune where poison ivy was rampant. She requested permission from the local conservation commission to remove the plants and replace them with other native species. This was easier said than done. Mechanical removal was the only efficient method and care had to be exercised extracting the poison ivy while minimizing damage to the dune. Poison ivy is very effective at controlling dune erosion.

And that is another important point when considering this plant invader. While poisonous to humans, there are over fifty species of birds (including pheasants) that consume the fruits. In addition, the thickets of poison ivy provide shelter from predators for many animals including rabbits.

This is the one plant that every casual hiker, walker, and observer must pay attention to. It's amazing to look up at a tall tree and see a poison ivy vine sending out its aerial rootlets all the way to the canopy. Admire it from a distance. Wariness and caution are advisable when confronting this plant invader.

While the dunes on the Cape are characterized by a variety of plant species, including beach grass, bayberry, and seaside rose, there is a plant invader that is increasingly seen. Spotted knapweed (*Centaurea biebersteinii*), one of the most invasive plants in the western part of the United States, is now commonly seen here. Not only is this plant growing along the sides of the road and disturbed areas, but it can be found competing with the essential beach grass on dunes.

Spotted knapweed is a member of the composite family, the Asteraceae. Related to dandelions and daisies, it has many similar characteristics of these familiar plants. Introduced from Europe in the 1800's, it now covers millions of acres in western states such as Montana and Idaho. It is included on the Massachusetts prohibited plant list which means it may not be sold or deliberately distributed in the state.

The plant can be easily identified. The flower head is pinkish-purple and looks a little like a thistle. The bracts have a blackish tinge to them. The plant grows one to four feet high with alternate, compound leaves. It also has a two to four foot taproot which allows it to grow in dry, sandy habitats.

Like so many weedy species, spotted knapweed produces thousands of seeds that are easily distributed by the wind. This biennial plant can quickly colonize an area and spread its population. Very few herbivores like to eat this plant, although there are a couple of seed head fly species that have been used in biological controls.

What makes this plant difficult to control as an invader is its ability to release a toxin called catechin into the soil. Catechin is a very effective substance that prevents other plants from growing by reducing their ability to absorb nutrients. Spotted knapweed does not reabsorb the chemical so it is able to grow without any interference. Combined with its strong taproot and enormous seed production, it is a very formidable plant invader.

As is true with most invasive species, spotted knapweed is an environmental problem. A reduction in plant diversity also reduces the diversity of animals that depend on plants for food and shelter. In a place like a sand dune, spotted knapweed is less effective than beach grass for controlling erosion. This could have an impact on many issues from endangered bird habitat to coastal property protection.

The use of herbicides creates its own set of environmental problems and has had limited success. Mechanically removing the entire plant prior to seed production is effective, but quite labor intensive. One must time it correctly as well. The seeds can remain viable in the soil for many years.

It is probably impossible to completely control this invader. However, selective and targeted areas could be managed, particularly where it may be competing with more desirable or even threatened plant species.

The most notorious plant invader on Cape Cod is undoubtedly the common reed (*Phragmites australis*). This tall, common grass grows around freshwater, brackish water, and even salt marsh systems. It is extremely invasive and often outcompetes all other plants in its path.

The density of this plant can be astounding. My students have measured over fifty plants per square meter in parts of Scorton Creek, Sandwich. They also determined that it has a high tolerance for changes in salinity and they measured dense growths in salinities as high as fifteen parts per thousand. That's about half the salinity of ocean water. Probably the most important fact is that no other plant species can survive in the habitats that *Phragmites* has colonized.

The common reed can grow over twelve feet high. Its hollow stems grow quickly from an underground rhizome. A quick scan around a dense population of reed can reveal new stem growth along the edges. In this way *Phragmites* continues its incessant march into an area. The plant also grows a productive terminal and feathery inflorescence. The developed seeds are easily distributed by the wind.

It's difficult to determine any use for this plant. I have observed red-winged blackbirds hiding in the reed thickets. One can see how small animals might find shelter within. Humans have used this plant in the past as a thatch for homes. Possibly it could be used as a source of biofuel in the future.

However, most efforts are directed towards removing and controlling this plant. Burning is useless as it only stimulates new growth. Mechanical removal is extremely problematic. The most effective means of controlling its spread is to open up the marshes so

Phragmites (top) encroaching on cattails in the Great Marsh, West Barnstable

that sea water enters the system. Higher levels of salinity will destroy the *Phragmites* growing along the edges. Several marsh systems have been successfully restored on the Cape using this method.

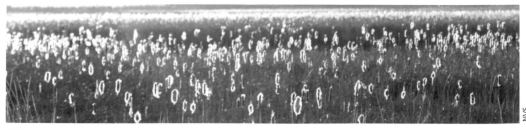

Sometimes plants are imported from other parts of the world and grown for ornamental purposes. They may even be beneficial to wildlife, producing edible fruit and providing needed shelter. However, because they are an introduced species, they can quickly invade a region and displace native species. One such plant is the multi-flora rose (*Rosa multiflora*). Though this is mainly a terrestrial plant, I have seen it as a major part of the vegetation near the edges of the marine environment.

Photo: James R. Brown

Like most roses the flower is attractive. It exists as groups of white flowers with bright yellow stamens. Round red fruit will appear in the summer. This plant is sometimes called the hedge rose because of its growth habit which can form dense shrubs with sharp thorns. It can also grow up the sides of fences and trees.

This plant presumably arrived from Japan in the 19th century. We can blame the popularity of roses for this introduction. Many varieties of roses from around the world have been introduced to brighten up our gardens. Unfortunately, this species will quickly crowd out any other plants in a garden.

It can be controlled by removing the entire plant including its root system. This is not an easy task and should be done with the young plant. A large population can only be removed with the assistance of heavy machinery.

The Values of Eelgrass

Throughout the region there are many rich ecosystems referred to as estuaries. This is where freshwater from rivers, streams and groundwater mix with the ocean's tides. These ecosystems are very diverse and productive and support large numbers of marine plants and animals. Nutrients tend to accumulate in their shallow waters and animals that are adapted to changing conditions feed and reproduce in these coastal areas. They also provide shelter and protection from storms and strong waves.

Estuaries contribute significant habitat for the one true marine flowering plant, namely eelgrass (*Zostera marina*), that is extremely important to many animal populations. Eelgrass is a member of the family Zosteraceae and forms large beds in subtidal shallow waters up and down the Atlantic coastline.

During the 1930's this plant was ravaged by an aquatic fungus or slime mold (*Labryrinthula zosterae*) and the majority of its population disappeared. Some areas did not recover for several decades from this wasting disease. In recent years eelgrass has faced additional environmental stressors. These include algae population blooms from nitrogen loading, the effects of overdevelopment on the coast, and the impact of hydraulic dredging of shellfish.

Eelgrass is a flowering plant and not a seaweed. It produces flowers and seeds and has vascular tissue for the transport of sugars, minerals and water through the plant. The blades grow from a sheath and the plant is attached by a strong root system as well as an underground stem known as a rhizome. It can reproduce both sexually and vegetatively. The plants can grow in extensive mats and are ecologically important to several marine animal species. These include many commercially important species such as scallops, flounder, blue mussels, oysters, black sea bass and blue crabs. Many other species including several worms, sea urchins and horseshoe crabs can also be located in an eelgrass bed. This small ecosystem also contains sponges, shrimp and bryozoans clinging to its blades. In addition to the economically important species mentioned earlier, there are pipefish, stickle-backs and mummichogs hiding in the eelgrass from predators.

The threats to the eelgrass beds and all of its inhabitants are numerous. Nitrogen runoff from septic systems, roads, and the atmosphere result in a rapid increase in some algae species such as sea lettuce (*Ulva lactuca*) or the oyster thief (*Codium fragile*). These algae grow rapidly in the presence of nitrogen and shade out the eelgrass beds below. This reduction in light intensity reduces the plant's ability to photosynthesize. Consequently it is weakened and unable to compete for the important sunlight that it needs. Some algae epiphytes grow extensively on the eelgrass blades, further reducing its photosynthetic capacity.

Because much of this nitrogen comes from human activity, increased development along the coast directly coincides with the loss of eelgrass. Runoff, erosion and increased sedimentation are a major problem for shallow bodies of water in areas of extensive development. The consequences include a reduction in the dependent animal populations such as scallops. So there are economic impacts from these environmental changes as well.

Eelgrass beds are additional buffers to strong wave action. In conjunction with salt marsh grasses, which often encircle an estuary, eelgrass can contribute to the stability of the area. This protects upland regions from erosion. Short term economic gains from activities such as dredging can have negative long term effects on adjacent properties and can cause a reduction in harvestable species.

Conservation measures are being taken to preserve these valuable habitats for shellfish and other species. Monitoring of water quality and eelgrass growth is essential to begin the restoration effort. If the stressor is reduced or removed, then it is possible to transplant eelgrass and begin the recovery of the system. However the reestablishment of productive eelgrass beds is not easy and will require a long term commitment with extensive research.

The author viewing eelgrass

On Golden Dune

Autumn is a time when the northeast forests are ablaze with color from the changing foliage. Most of the summer wildflowers have disappeared and signs of dormancy begin to appear in the dominant vegetation.

But there are still bright flowers to be seen. One grows right next to the ocean's edge. Seaside goldenrod (*Solidago sempervirens*) exhibits its bright yellow flowerheads on the coastal sand dunes right up to November. Growing on a tall stem of three to six feet, the flowers of seaside goldenrod are conspicuous and clustered. The alternate leaves are evergreen and larger toward the base of the plant. This native wildflower is perennial and grows in the sandy soil where it is also resistant to coastal wind and salt spray.

Seaside goldenrod is a member of the very diverse family called the Asteraceae. Only the orchid family has more species than this group. And there are many familiar relatives of goldenrod including daisies, dandelions, and asters. The Asteraceae, which is also called the sunflower family, used to be named the Compositae. That is because the flower in this group really consists of a composite of two kinds of flowers. Inside the inflorescence are tiny disk flowers. These are surrounded by petal-like ray flowers. So the flower on goldenrod is, in fact, a head of several small ray and disk flowers. The fruit is called an achene and contains a single seed which is distributed by the wind.

Seaside goldenrod is an ecologically important plant. It is a common member of the assemblage of dune plant species which collectively reduce erosion of the dune from wind and storms. This is a noninvasive species so it can be planted in these fragile areas. All goldenrods are often mistakenly accused of causing hayfever and other allergies. But look closely at the plant. They are often visited by large numbers of pollinating bees. With insect vectors as pollinators, the pollen is not blowing around in the wind. The real culprit is most likely ragweed (*Ambrosia*) that flowers around the same time as goldenrod and is wind pollinated.

Photo: Audrey Russano

Goldenrods are not the easiest plants to identify to species. There are over 100 species and many of them hybridize. On the other hand seaside goldenrod is noted for its habitat preferences. It can grow along the edges of salt marshes and sand dunes. It grows closer to the ocean than any of the other common goldenrod species in this region. It's a hardy coastal plant that adds color to the shoreline, supports the stability of dunes, and helps sustain a healthy bee population.

Gardening by the Coast

The arrival of spring brings out the gardeners throughout the region. Flowers and vegetables appear. Lawns turn green. Trees and shrubs begin to leaf out. Before you commit yourself to a particular scheme, why not consider ways of providing a natural, sustainable landscape? The application of ecological landscaping has enormous implications for a coastline. Sensitive coastal areas are subject to water quality issues partially associated with landscaping practices. The excess use of fertilizers can have a serious impact on the health of coastal bays and estuaries.

The overuse of nitrogen and the subsequent growth of algae can accelerate a process called eutrophication. The nitrogen comes from a variety of sources including septic systems, the atmosphere, and lawn fertilizers. When a single species of algae such as sea lettuce (*Ulva lactuca*) suddenly increases in population, it blocks sunlight to other plants including the ecologically important eelgrass (*Zostera marina*). Bacteria are responsible for the

sea lettuce

decomposition of algae. This process can happen very quickly. For example, sea lettuce only lives for a few weeks. During decomposition the bacteria consume oxygen, creating low dissolved oxygen concentrations for invertebrates and fish. Crabs, shrimp, mollusks and small fish can be killed under these conditions. So finding attractive plants that minimize the need for fertilizers can help reduce nitrogen loading in marine waters.

The use of native species has many benefits to the coastline. These plants are well adapted to the seasons and require minimal maintenance. They also attract several species of wildlife, thus increasing biological diversity, always a good thing for the environment. In other words, they help stabilize an ecosystem more effectively than one or two dominant invasive plants. Of course what most homeowners want is an attractive place, one that they can enjoy throughout the year. By using ecological planning for a garden, you can enhance its beauty and attractiveness while protecting the diverse plant and animal marine communities that are essential to our local environment and economy.

Some common plant species can be quite attractive in a garden. Dusty miller (*Artemisia stelleriana*) is a pale green perennial plant that grows primarily on dunes and sandy soil. The leaves are covered with small white hairs and are round at the tips. They grow close to the ground and function effectively in preventing erosion from wind and storms. Flowers are small and yellow on a tall stalk and are wind-pollinated. These plants are grown mainly for their foliage.

bearberry

One of my favorites is bearberry (*Arctostaphylos uva-ursi*), an indigenous evergreen groundcover. This plant has thick, dark green leaves, small cup-shaped white flowers, and red berries that are popular with birds. It grows in sandy soil and is quite effective in controlling erosion. It may also grow with another red-berried plant called wintergreen (*Gaultheria procumbens*) whose white flowers are bell-shaped. The leaves are oval and shiny green, and produce the characteristic wintergreen odor. This can be detected by smelling a torn leaf.

40

Interspersed with these species in the same sandy habitat is the taller broom crowberry (*Corema conradii*). These plants also form large mats and the flowers are light pink. Look closely at the leaves however. They are quite different from bearberry and are shaped as needles, almost conifer-like. The berries are dark purple, another distinguishing characteristic.

Attractive trees that could be planted include the American holly (*Ilex opaca*). Their glossy green leaves contain a number of spines on the margins and this plant can easily grow in sandy soil of the Cape. These trees have separate sexes with the red berries appearing on the female.

A widely distributed tree in this area is the Eastern red cedar (*Juniperus virginiana*). This medium-sized conifer grows from 20 to 40 feet high. The leaves are scale-like and the branches may have several blue berries which are actually cones. The bark is reddish-brown. This tree often grows in rows where the seeds were distributed by birds.

The seaside rose (*Rosa rugosa*) was introduced to this country in the late 1800's and is often used in landscaping throughout the Cape. Though this plant has the potential to be invasive, it can be controlled with proper management. Rugosa means wrinkled which describes the surface of the leaf. The plant has a compound leaf with five to nine leaflets. The flowers are red, pink, or white and appear in late spring through the fall. The plant grows as a shrub up to five feet tall and produces the fleshy fruits called rose hips which can be made into jelly.

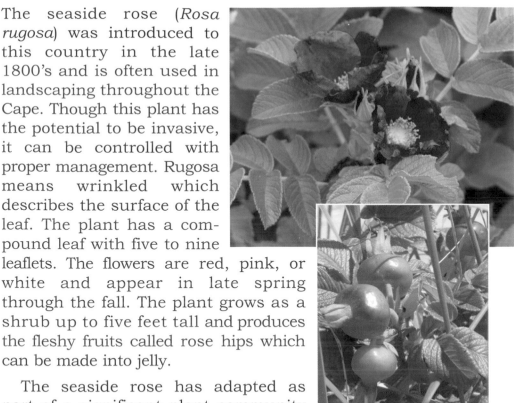

The seaside rose has adapted as part of a significant plant community on a sand dune, protecting the coastline from erosion by blocking the removal of sand. It adds diversity to this assemblage of salt-tolerant, xerophytic (desert loving) plants. Not only is it a food source for animals, but its dense branches provide shelter.

One of my favorite and hardy plant species is beach heather or poverty grass (*Hudsonia tomentosa*), a conspicuous, low-growing, grayish-green shrub. This plant is neither a heather nor a grass. It belongs to the rockrose family, the Cistaceae. *Hudsonia* is an excellent erosion control agent on dunes. Its deep roots and spreading growth habit help block the removal of sand by wind and rain. It is adapted to this harsh,

dry environment and is able to capture and conserve water. From a distance beach heather appears to grow in dense mats on the sand. A close examination of the leaves reveals a scale-like and alternate arrangement. In early summer it produces an array of small golden flowers that open in the sun. There are five petals and 5-30 stamens. The plant is evergreen and perennial.

Not all invasive plants are unwelcome in the garden. One very persistent, yet attractive species is yarrow (*Archillea millefolium*), a member of the Compositae family. This herbaceous perennial grows abundantly along the edges of gardens wherever there is space to conquer. It is easily identified by its fernlike leaves which arc highly dissected into numerous leaflets, and its white, sometimes yellow, flowers. The plants don't usually grow more than a couple of feet tall, particularly because they seem to crowd each other for the limited space. Consequently they can function as a good ground cover if the space is not needed for other plants. Yarrow starts to appear in gardens in June and will last through late September. It grows best in full sun and does quite well in the sandy soil. Fertilizing this plant is unnecessary.

Yarrow is often cited as an important medicinal herb which has been used widely for many centuries. It apparently has been applied to numerous ailments including headaches, nosebleeds and fevers. Today it is more likely used in dried flower arrangements or as borders for different gardens. I have used it sparingly with other container plants, giving a nice green outline to the various flowers in the pot.

Ecologically yarrow has many benefits. In addition to its role of controlling erosion as a ground cover, it can attract beneficial garden insects such as lady bugs. It makes a nice border around other plants, but does require some work in keeping it under control.

The Jellies

In recent years there have been reports of large swarms of jellyfish in southern waters, getting tangled in fishermen's nets, as well as washing ashore. Warnings have been issued in places such as Hawaii and Japan about encountering stinging jellyfish on the beaches. Several animals collected seem to be larger than normal, feeding on the constant nutrients flowing from land.

The jellyfish belong to the phylum Cnidaria which also includes the coral and the freshwater hydras. There does appear to be an increase in jellyfish populations around the world. Some speculate that this rise in jellies is due to climate change. A warmer ocean creates ideal conditions for jellyfish survival. These animals appear to be better adapted to higher nutrient concentrations, including the subsequent drop in dissolved oxygen as algae blooms occur. Large populations of jellyfish can easily consume many of the eggs and larvae of fish species. Not only do jellyfish increase in population under these conditions, but they may also increase in size when feeding in areas of sewage and other pollution runoff. We usually suspect an environmental problem when a species suddenly declines. However, as we can see with the jellyfish, an increase also serves as an environmental signal that something is wrong.

On Cape Cod jellyfish are mainly confined to the warmer months of the year. The most common species is the moon jelly (*Aurelia aurita*). This animal is a few inches in length and has four pinkish gonads in its clear center. The body is bell-shaped and moves by forcing water out of its body. In fact the animal lacks circulatory, respiratory, or excretory systems. Like most jellyfish it has tentacles with stinging cells called nematocysts. Moon jellies feed on plankton. They have both a sessile polyp stage and a motile medusa stage.

The moon jelly is harmless to humans, but there is another species which is quite dangerous and should be avoided. Though not common here, the Portuguese man-of-war (*Physalia physalia*) occasionally arrives on the Cape via the Gulf Stream. This mainly tropical, jellyfish-like species was first seen by English sailors traveling around Portugal. It can be found throughout the world and is a menace to marathon swimmers. Its nematocysts are very effective in paralyzing its prey such as small fish. The difference here is that these tentacles can stretch as long as 50 feet.

A swimmer might be able to avoid the floating sail of the animal at the surface of the water, but could easily come into contact with the trailing tentacles. And that could prove to be fatal. The stinging cells are very strong and toxic. It is one of the most poisonous animals in the ocean. Large welts will appear on the skin of the victim if contact is made. Even if washed up on a beach, the animal retains its toxicity for a long time.

I know someone who went into a coma after touching the tentacles of a beached man-of-war. Fortunately he survived the ordeal.

The animal is identified by its bluish-pink float (pneumatophore) which functions like a sail and is steered by the wind. Of course the animal also travels in currents, such as the Gulf Stream, and ends up in colder waters such as Cape Cod and the Islands. The float is filled with gases and can be around one foot long.

What is really fascinating about the man-of-war is that it is an example of a colonial animal, consisting of many individuals with a division of labor, yet functioning as a single animal. These individuals, or polyps, have specialized functions such as feeding, reproduction, or defense. When they feed, the entire colony benefits. Not all animals are adversely affected by man-of-war. Sea turtles nibble on the tentacles with no effects. There is also a small fish called *Nomeus* which is unaffected by the stinging cells. *Nomeus* may even assist the man-of-war by attracting other fish into the trap.

Sightings of the Portuguese man-of-war in the northeast are rare. Still they have been seen in recent years on several beaches. This situation will probably occur again as surface sea temperatures continue to rise. No one really knows all the implications of climate change, but it does seem possible that more species that are normally found in tropical waters will find their way to the shoreline of Cape Cod.

A Tale of Three Animals

The winter beach may appear barren and bare of any marine life. Broken shells and a bit of seaweed may be the only signs of life. However, visit a rocky substrate such as a jetty and you may observe a huge colony of northern rock barnacles (*Semibalanus balanoides*). The barnacle is the only crustacean that stays in place for its entire adult life. The initial problem is getting established, therefore large numbers of barnacles live next to each other. Barnacles tend to settle and grow in areas that are already barnacle colonies. During reproduction the fertilized eggs develop into larvae that swim, grow and molt. These young larvae are called cyprids and will settle by cementing themselves on a suitable substrate. A barnacle will spend its adult life in an upside down position, its head cemented to a rock while moving its feathery legs to capture small food particles.

Barnacle feeding schedules are determined by the tides. At high tide the legs are beating in the water, trapping phytoplankton, while at low tide they close, protecting the animal within from desiccation. The largest barnacles may have several white plates that grow over each other. They grow their exoskeleton by molting. In addition to rock jetties, barnacles can also be found attached to other animals such as spider crabs and horseshoe crabs. Barnacles are also very competitive with other colonizers including blue mussels and rockweed for the limited space on a jetty. Because of these biological pressures and the physical impact of wave action, their populations exist in patches on the rock surface.

One of the most intriguing and often overlooked animals is the tubeworm *Spirorbis borealis* which lives attached to the surface of rockweed (*Fucus vesiculosus*) and eel grass (*Zostera marina*). Animals that are attached to the surface of a host such as a plant are called ectosymbionts. Examine the blades of rockweed to see this tiny animal. You will observe a series of coiled tubes in rows. These polychaete worms remove calcium carbonate (lime) from the water to form their tubes which range from 2-4 mm long.

The animals are hermaphroditic and release their eggs into the water after a period of brooding in the tube. The young swimming

larvae quickly organize their tubes and attach to a rockweed. Like the barnacle they can exist in enormous numbers and it is easy to find discarded rockweed in the wrack line covered with them.

Fucus with tube worms

Spirorbus is a consumer and uses its feathery tentacles to filter feed small planktonic cells in the water. There are many species worldwide.

Spirorbus is eaten by those organisms that graze on the algae. Use a hand lens to observe the details of this interesting animal.

One of the most commonly misidentified organisms at the beach is *Bugula turrita*. At first glance it looks like a small clump of brown seaweed, but in reality it's an animal and belongs to the bryozoan group. This colonial animal is composed of individuals called zooids that have specialized functions such as feeding and reproduction. These zooids collectively obtain nutrition by using their tentacles to filter plankton from the water.

Bugula is a common fouling organism and often grows on the bottom of boats, docks and pilings. It frequently washes up on beaches in large clumps where it gets stranded in the wrack line. It's this appearance that gives it the name of moss animal. This bushy animal grows up to 15 cm tall and can also attach to shells and algae.

Ocean Death Traps

Plastic bags that look like jellyfish. Six-pack rings that trap helpless birds. Fishing gear that surrounds trapped whales. Small plastic pellets that clog the intestines of birds and mammals. These are just some of the items floating in the ocean that endanger many marine life forms every day.

Marine debris is a serious problem in all parts of the ocean. Consider some of the staggering statistics.

According to the National Academy of Science, around 14 billion pounds of garbage are dumped in the ocean each year. That is equivalent to around 1.5 million pounds per hour. Each day over 650,000 bottles end up in the ocean. Up to 100,000 miles of fishing nets are lost throughout the world's ocean every year. When you consider that the United States uses more than 100 billion plastic bags a year and that these can create a hazard in the environment, you begin to see the magnitude of the problem. Most of these bags are thrown away, yet we know there is no "away". They have to go somewhere and that place is often the ocean. Some estimates are that each bag takes about two decades to break down in the environment, though some reports are for much longer. They become death traps for marine animals such as sea turtles which mistakenly see them as jellyfish, a favorite food item. Many of the endangered sea turtles have plastic in their digestive tracts.

50

The impact on wildlife is distressing. Thousands of pelagic birds, seals, turtles and whales have died through entanglement, starvation, and injury. Some of these animals ingest the plastic in the form of small pellets, thus clogging their intestines and resulting in starvation. Many others get entangled by soda rings, monofilament lines, and packing materials. They die from exhaustion, drowning, or infection.

One of the most insidious effects of oceanic plastic is their degradation into tiny particles which enter the plankton. These plastic pieces are consumed by many animals and may influence the food web. These small particles of plastic may also absorb and concentrate poisons such as pesticides from the environment. In other words filter-feeding animals as well as larger fish may be ingesting plastic instead of nutritious food. It's possible that these organisms could suffer from starvation as a result.

Where does the trash come from? The garbage gets dumped from boats or blows into coastal waters from land. It's hard to imagine why anyone would deliberately dump plastics overboard, or leave their trash in the sand, but the sad truth is that it happens quite often. It is illegal to dump plastics in American waters but you can imagine the difficulty in enforcing the ban.

Education and conservation seem to be the answers to this international problem. Many people are unaware that these products can do much harm and there has to be a continuous ongoing effort to inform the public. With so many consumer products using plastic, including excessive wrapping, it is necessary to embark on educational campaigns for their proper use and disposal.

Another important step that can be taken is to simply reduce the amount of plastic consumed. Most plastics can be recycled which has the added benefit of reducing fossil fuel consumption as they are all products of petroleum. If each of us carefully considers what we consume and tries to eliminate the excess of plastic from our lives, we will help protect marine species.

The Return to Crocker Neck

It's the end of another year and the weather is very mild for Cape Cod in winter. For several decades I have walked the trails around the Crocker Neck Salt Marsh Conservation Area in Barnstable and I have chronicled this area in *The Ecology of a Cape Cod Salt Marsh.* I visit this beautiful marsh at least twice a week and so I've become familiar with the subtle and seasonal changes of this dynamic system.

Today a heavy fog is shrouding Poponessett Bay, making it practically invisible. The water's edge is calm and peaceful. I surprise a wading great blue heron who quickly flies away, squawking and protesting 'til he's a safe distance away. The cordgrass is golden brown and matted in places subject to high tides, waves, and wind. The remains of a few marine animals are scattered on the small sandy beach. The broken shell of a quahog, the claw of a blue crab, and the carapace of a horseshoe crab lay entangled in a mat of eel grass and rockweed.

It's raining slightly, though I hardly notice. The foliose lichens on the pitch pines seem to glisten more brightly as they absorb the moisture from the air. Long gone are the bright flowers of summer including the purple sea lavender that line the edge of the marsh, the orange milkweed along the trail, and the numerous white and yellow asters.

Yet when I look carefully I can still observe some remnants of color along the trails. These are the shiny red berries on the wintergreen and bearberry ground cover plants. Other fruits become more visible such as the grayish clusters of poison ivy, the dried brown fruits of sumac, and the blackish-purple berries lingering on greenbrier.

wintergreen

Though most of the plants have lost their leaves, a distinct zonation can still be seen around the marsh. Following the tall cordgrass by the water's edge, a large meadow of brown salt marsh hay makes up the bulk of the marsh. The upper regions are characterized by a row of spike grass and black grass. Small dry populations of sea pickle, sea lavender, and salt marsh asters are scattered throughout the salt marsh hay. The entire marsh is surrounded by groundsel and marsh elder shrubs.

Because of the mild and moist conditions, three small earth stars have emerged from the soil on a path through a grove of pine trees. These fungi are a kind of puffball and their center is swollen with spores ready to be released in the rain and wind. I leave them alone in hopes that they will be successful in their productivity and that other earth stars will grow in this area again.

I am still waiting for this year's first snowfall. Though late in the season I know it will inevitably occur and the muted dormancy now seen throughout Crocker Neck will metamorphose into a deep slumber. This marsh is beautiful at any time of the year, but the resting stage known as winter carries with it the hope of renewal and growth that will once again emerge a few months from now.

"We need to feel
the sand on our feet,
the wind at our backs,
and the smell of the salt in the air."

Deborah Shiflett-Fitton

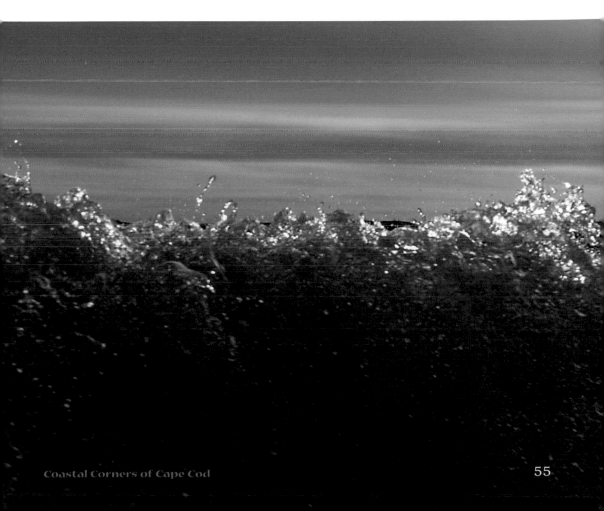

Recommended References

Barbo, Theresa Mitchell. **Cape Cod Wildlife**. History Press. Charleston, SC. 2012.

Carson, Rachel. **The Edge of the Sea**. Houghton Mifflin Company. Boston, MA. 1955.

Hay, John and Peter Farb. **The Atlantic Shore**. Harper Colophon Books. New York and Evanston. 1966.

Louv, Richard. **Last Child in the Woods**. Algonquin Books of Chapel Hill, NC. 2008.

Newton, Gilbert. **Discovering the Cape Cod Shoreline**. West Barnstable Press, MA. 2012.

Newton, Gilbert. **Seaweeds of Cape Cod Shores**. Cape Cod Museum of Natural History. West Barnstable Press, MA. 2008.

Petry, Loren C. and Marcia G. Norman. **A Beachcomber's Botany**. The Chatham Conservation Foundation, Inc. Fifth Edition, Chatham, MA. 1982.

Waller, Geoffrey, Ed. **Sealife - A Complete Guide to the Marine Environment**. Smithsonian Institution Press. Washington, D.C. 1996.

Zim, Herbert S. and Lester Ingle. **Seashore Life**. St. Martin's Press. New York. 1989.

The Author

Gilbert Newton is a Cape Cod native who has been teaching environmental science at Sandwich High School and the Cape Cod Community College for many years. His classes include coastal ecology, botany, horticulture, coastal zone management, and environmental technology. In 2013 he became the first Director of the Sandwich School District's STEM Academy. He completed his graduate work in biology at Florida State University. Gil is one of the founders of the Barnstable Land Trust and past president of the Thornton W. Burgess Society and of the Association to Preserve Cape Cod. He is the author of *Seaweeds of Cape Cod Shores, The Ecology of a Cape Cod Salt Marsh,* and *Discovering the Cape Cod Shoreline.*

The Photographer

Chris Dumas has lived and worked on Cape Cod for many years. He teaches earth and space science at Sandwich High School. Chris has been involved with outdoor education for most of his career. Photography has been an important part of Chris' life for the last decade and he has traveled around the country in search of interesting vistas. Chris has a graduate degree in Resource Conservation from the University of Montana and is a native of the St. Lawrence River Valley region of New York. His photography can also be seen in *The Ecology of a Cape Cod Salt Marsh* and *Discovering the Cape Cod Shoreline.*

This book was designed and typeset by Nancy Viall Shoemaker of West Barnstable Press, West Barnstable, Massachusetts. The text font is Bookman Old Style, designed by Alexander Phemister in 1858, working from the font Caslon. It was constructed with straighter serifs, allowing it to keep its readability at small sizes. Photo credits were set in Frutiger, designed by Swiss typographer Adrian Frutiger (1928-). The font used for the chapter heads is Nueva. It was designed by Carol Twombly for Adobe in 1994. *Coastal Corners of Cape Cod* was printed on 100 lb. white matte stock with a 12 pt. laminated cover.

Entire book, including cover, printed on recycled paper

Photo: Nancy Viall Shoemaker